The Vigilant One

Acknowledgements are due to the following publications in which some of the poems first appeared: *Clochadóir, The Landscape Anthology, On The Counterscarp – An Anthology of Limerick Writing 1961-1991. The Stony Thursday Book/ Cuaderno de Madrid, The Limerick Poetry Broadsheet*, *Poetry Ireland Review, Cyphers, Quimper est Poesie No. 10, France*. Acknowledgement is also due to the Heinrich Böll Foundation for a residency in the Heinrich Böll Cottage, Achill, July 1994.

*To John
on our meeting*

Jo Slade

The Vigilant One

Jo Slade.

SALMON POETRY

Published in 1994 by
Salmon Publishing Ltd,
Upper Fairhill, Galway
A division of Poolbeg Enterprises Ltd

© Jo Slade 1994

The Publishers gratefully acknowledge the assistance of The Arts Council

The moral right of the author has been asserted.

A catalogue record for this book is available from the British Library.

ISBN 1 897648 32 4

All rights reserved. No part of this publication may be reproduced or transmitted in any form or by any means, electronic or mechanical, including photography, recording, or any information storage or retrieval system, without permission in writing from the publisher. The book is sold subject to the condition that it shall not, by way of trade or otherwise, be lent, resold or otherwise circulated without the publisher's prior consent in any form of binding or cover other than that in which it is published and without a similar condition, including this condition, being imposed on the subsequent purchaser.

Cover painting by Jo Slade
Cover design by Poolbeg Group Services Ltd
Set by Poolbeg Group Services Ltd in Palatino 11/15
Printed by Colour Books, Baldoyle Industrial Estate, Dublin 13

For John & David

Contents

I.
The Sailor

Everyday The Sky Opens 3
I Have Never Learned To Speak 5
Swimming 6
The Round World Is Poised Upon The Sea 7
The Sailor 8
White Crow 9
Instruments Of Measurement 10
It Is No Use To Wonder 11
Watch Me Wherever I Go 12
Homecoming: Up and Down an
  Octave in Nine Movements 13

II.
Waterfall

Reasons 21
The Vigilant One 23
Dream Of Destruction 25
Waterfall: The Song Of Kinapipi 26
Five Lines For Claire 28
Admiral 29
Night Pours Down 30

Contents

I
The Sailor

Everyday The Sky Opens	3
I Have Never Learned To Speak	5
Swimming	6
The Round World Is Poised Upon The Sea	7
The Sailor	8
White Crow	9
Instruments Of Measurement	10
It Is No Use To Wonder	11
Watch Me Wherever I Go	12
Homecoming: Up and Down an Octave in Nine Movements	13

II
Waterfall

Reasons	21
The Vigilant One	23
Dream Of Destruction	25
Waterfall. The Song Of Kunapipi	26
Five Lines For Clairr	28
Admiral	29
Night Pours Down	30

For Peru	31
Song For Small Nations	32
In Bosnia. 1993	33
The Rescuer	34

III
Innocence And Regret

Seven Times Crossed	39
In The Beginning There Was Chaos	41
Recollection Of A Dream	43
Out Of My Blue Mouth	44
White Bridge	45
The Tales Of Innocence And Regret	46
Fruit	
Wind	
Stones	
Grief	
Expulsion, A Foetal Hymn	50
Distance	52
A Limb Discarded	53
Trust My Fortification Of Stone	54

IV
Gericault

The Sky Sees All	57
In The Forest Snow Gathers	59
Snow Causes Eruptions	60

First There Is The Question Of Weight	61
What Cannot Be Seen	62
Believe Me There Is Only Wind	63
I Glimpsed The Moon	64
Eyes	66
The Singers Are Silent	68
Notes	70

I

The Sailor

Every day the sky opens
blue as my silk gown.
Morning of my life
there is joy when you
come as water comes
every day to the pier.

I Have Never Learned To Speak

I have never learned to speak.
See, my tongue is still,
see, my feet walk away
wild and solitary.

I have never learned to say
your name, it is so simple,
it is the same as putting
my hand across your face.

I have no one to talk to,
no sound to communicate.
When dogs dance
in celestial blackness

I shoot an arrow at the sun;
when the stag leaps out
I race him until daylight comes.
Then I am happy.

Swimming

I believe if I could swim with you
I would be really changed.
What is it that would be so different,
would my children know me
my face like a thousand fishes?

Deep in the earth's crust
our city is buried,
our city is the head of a whale,
so old it lies in cold water
among stones that sing,
among stones that have melody.

If I swam with you
what would they call me?
Me with change wrapped
round my shoulders.
If I was blind
by your hands spontaneous grasp
light would grow from me,
fishes would grow from me.

The Round World Is Poised Upon The Sea

The round world is poised upon the sea.
For six days I've watched it,
sat in the boatman's chair
and watched it from the shore.

This means nothing to me,
it's not prophetic.
What becomes of me is inconsequential,
in a sense I am forgotten.

The round world has not spoken,
for three days it is silent.
Where is he, the sad one
who's voice came across to me?

Is he lost, do his eyes
drift inside the ocean
and what do they see
drowned in deep water?
For me, judgement is torture.

Everything subsides,
eventually everything leaves –
voices, winds, oceans, pity.
For now, I'm content to be

daughter of a simple boatman,
to wear the conch
like an ear between my breasts,
to feel the sun's hot tongue
turn round me.

The Sailor

The sailor slept for forty days,
she slept through the turmoil of terrible times
she slept through high waves
and water blood coloured
she slept through wondrous days that loved her,
she could have conceived the world.
She breathed on great armies
and on soldiers that pranced the shore,
at night in darkness she crept the land
and what she said was barely heard, like a cloud.
Into men's heads her hand extended
but this was no gift or comfort,
day waited for her to come softly,
a bird rose out of the trenches.

White Crow

I will study the sky,
there where clouds go
I will be,

I will know names
like Hyades come from
the mountain,

I will watch at night
for Aquarius
water of gold,

I will wait
as cicadas do
for warm sun.

My song
will be pure
as a white crow.

Instruments Of Measurement

Because I have seen the sun and moon
because I am familiar with eccentric
movements in the sky
because I have spent my life inside
content with my instruments of measurement
telescopes and pens,
because it's to me her majesty attends
and loves me deeply,
because I am alone among women
and my isolation invents connections
and expansions so the earth grows
even as I remain within
its physical restrictions,
because I know (unbelievably)
how to acquire flight,
because I believe in something greater
how lonely I am and yet
such emptiness is of necessity just
because darkness converges
in my clenched fist and into
depths of sadness I descend,
a journeywoman on the twentieth step.

It Is No Use To Wonder

It is no use to wonder about me
or the river that passes my house
or the tree that is straight and bare
or the large orange moon
or my mother's white hair
or my child's azure eyes
or my lover's perfectly erect penis
or my sister's chestnut skin
or my hand that writes this poem

or my sadness
because I have lived with these things
a long time and I don't understand
but I keep their names
among my precious things.

Watch Me Wherever I Go

Watch me wherever I go
even into your breathing soul.
Don't love me the way you love songs
I am among friends ready
with fierce eyes to expose you.
Watch me in the shade of things,
weighed, books opened on the stand
hands numbed in fugitive shadow.

Homecoming : Up And Down An Octave In Nine Movements

1

Light in fields, soft translucent, moves across
    stealthily
light rises, creeps trees, enters inside, destroys
    darkness
as fire destroys trees –
trees wait for light to occur
light cheated
ingénue, young, never free –
nomadic wanders into shadow, across deserts
over hills mounds of bones, people buried in sand
sand covers their eyes.

2

Nomadic tribes trudge over me –
look for the brightest spot on the line
look for home
search the sea
light moves on
moves over me
chant psalms
I hear – I understand
sacred songs mother tongue
I am eager to understand, ready to be cheated
to die.

3

Lie love on the ground
I want to love you
turn around
your thighs of light glimmer
my tongue and the light on your hair,
in there like minute creatures like tiny eggs
Man Ray's tears
heavenly pearls of despair –
so love could you move me?

4

I hear your pulse
pray we can
up to the stars
to Jupiter burnt
to us like trees that light has entered
destroyed –
look for home
now is the time for home
where you used to be – in a chair
smoke rises
something burns beneath the tree
you burn
waiting for me to come.

5

Morning light
time to go
home across deserts
to find home
over bones crunched under pale skies waiting for
light
to rise
to devour deep blue
seas of porpoises
I want to swim
pull me along – through water
turn
near now I'm near to light
come love
let me guide you
to nowhere – for nothing
forever,
into the bleak line
over the sea and sand
outside the sea children die
leaves glide down, trample on
trudge
children my children alone in the sand
mysteries I don't understand,
their tiny feet move over me
nomadic forever
for nothing
looking for home
for the brightest star, for glimmers on the horizon
waiting for skies to change.

6

I love you through and through
now sand sculpted eyes rise
move me
what moves you?
My love – my children do they move you?
Alone in the sand waiting for their Da
looking to the sea
to the porpoises
blue
clear like eyes opened in sleep
or mornings early
so blue
like dolphins that bring you when they look for you
for their Da
coming over deserts, over mounds of bones
looking for home
now, it's home.

7

Were you cheated too?
For my love I would die
for my children I stay alive
and wait like the white moon
cycle after cycle
alone among trees
up to my neck in sand
in mysteries I don't understand.

8

Nomadic lovers wander
search night into night for childlike faces in the dawn
on the sea
hear cries
high pitched in water
I could find my children if they were two hundred miles
   away
I hear wind whisper in despair
and my love in winter
in high seas
looking for home
now is the time for home
light fades under trees
burnt wood devours the black that you carry
water bearer come from the sea
young lad lied to,
young woman full of dance
children lied to
all going home alone
nomadic over deserts – over hills
looking for home, for light
like dawn on dolphins – blue –
clear as pure pearls
Man Ray's tears of despair.

9

I am prepared for my journey
for my love I would die
for my children I stay alive
and wait for light
looking for home
now is the time for home.
Stay alive even after dusk when all light is gone
listen for their whispers
looking to the water
looking for their Da
coming over deserts
over mounds
waiting for me to come
and my children
awed by the light
by the dolphins
home going after love making
by the light of a moon
cycle after cycle
going home.

II

Waterfall

Now there are reasons
for the unleashing of words
torrents of speech fall into
the pool – all in a moment
we change we have found
our own tongues we can
explore faces and hands.

The Vigilant One

Would I stay here because all that I know is here?
The sky its sheer width and rain falling
and wind coming over the water to meet me
walking alone always keeping watch for a sign.

Would I stay here fear hovering over me,
sometimes unutterable as silence
sometimes large as a March moon
and would you stay here with me?

You, shadow across a mountain, slit
in an angry stone where rare blooms cluster
nothing inane my spirit open to all I see.
Stay with me my friend of all these years

purled in green fields white grass wavers
the morning light stark upon me
like madness roaming in from the sea.
If I try to think deeper with you listening

there is no real love only the insistence
of the soul only the need to hear another's
voice here, now, in the silence of passing,
to be the audible shadow of substance

to be absolutely and then knowing nothing
to be dust blown into a footprint –
the lodged dirt of another's journey,
where you go I go to mark your way

to say it's all to nowhere and never
go alone and never stay longer than the waves.
See, inside the lighted window they love desperately
they want to extinguish the malicious hour,

we are no better now for all our nights and days,
no one stays and no one gets away.
Listen, the wind's persistence a baleful tone
see, that perch where no birds land

where black leaves thieve from darkness
and cloak in bleak disguise the grief of the world.
I will stay, until life tires me
makes me old and water flows over me

and I swallow the sky and old sirens sing for me.
What keeps me then and what is best for me
to watch the clouds my life among the trees?
And I the endlessly abiding swan, the one

who loves for what if not for love itself.
My hour was long before I saw her wings open
and pure snow merged into grey, before
I learned to say, I am I was and I will be.

Dream Of Destruction

When we have destroyed the city
let us move upstream
and burn the temple.
Then take the trembling bell

to the wood, dig deep
bury it in damp mud.
What could be greater than fire?
The tree absorbed by flame

the pliant earth's scorched
surface all remain as witness,
nothing defies the sun.
This is the saddest place

I've passed through,
another fragile effigy
this beleaguered city
to which we've come.

Soon there will be nothing left,
not an image saved that could
be used to make a poem, a song
for my dream of destruction.

Waterfall. The Song Of Kunapipi

When the wall is finished
raise a tent for me,
a kind of shield to cover me.
Assign two swans as sentinels
and have Abu come
with fresh milk at dawn,
he will tell me of the city.
Tell my sister Soluma
it is eight weeks
since our last meeting,
I miss her terribly.
Please, tell her I pray
every night for her
for Soluma there is
a new star and in the day
all that is golden blue
belongs to her.
The crude songs they sing
these men who have come
to trade, three times
they've returned,
they refuse to listen
they accuse me of destruction.
They say a rainbow serpent
hides in my womb
and from my mouth
comes the sound of a lizard.
So long now since speech

came as it used to
with the sun and rain,
so long again
since what must be said
became a dove curled
on my tongue –
see how it flew from my mouth
and the way the world received it.
In the waterfall at Sion Creek
there are more words
than you can speak –
certainly when snow melts
in the mountain
a great rush of speech
can be heard in the water.
What does it say,
what does the water say
to the clear sky that lays
down on its surface?
Everything becomes accepted,
even after time,
everything becomes
what it should be.
We become what is ours
from the beginning.
Even before speech
I was something.
High in the cool mountain
lives my name –
solitary sound of rain,
colour of water hyacinths
that line the river.

Five Lines For Clairr

There seems a sky of crushed roses
red and white
and waters salubrious beneath
an aqua green
as leaves fallen into time.

Admiral

Odour of time in change
the bleached winged
remain to die
or overwinter as larvae.

The simple altruism
of butterflies,
light beam scintilla
caught glowing

right across the field,
no mowing now the aspen
grass has grown,
tickled at the roots

it sways in and out
of shade, all this lingers,
the sky a crude blue
permanent as earth and air

and through it all
the resonant pincall
of the Admiral.

Night Pours Down

Night pours down,
a stream of stars wavers.
This is the world
before light or breath.

Cowed under,
earth watches through
its soft eyes covered
in cloth of dreams.

Light in water
rushes beneath wind,
look deeper in –
time goes,

as if at its end
it began again,
so like water
this stream of life,

so like earth
that waits
our nights pass.

For Peru

I promise you, today at 10.40 pm
I am crying for you –
and for your wonderful hills
and for your buoyant tears
that float above the cities.

Let us say goodbye
to floating islands
of guidebooks, to animal
tourists, to the gluttonous
astronaut high on your
octane air, let us look
for your children
and when you pray
let your wailing prayer
resound in the mountain
and let your God fear,
'Oh condorcito, condorcito.'

Do you hear, wings
out there in the dark?
Sometimes the bird comes,
then God means no more
than a dead radio
and our tears are wasted.

Song For Small Nations

A wren pierced in the heart
by a soldier's cruel spear
had been singing, clear
as the day it was born,
I listened to its song.

Everywhere there are Samurais,
even in our dreams –
everywhere there are soldiers
who want to crush our hands
and sew our lips like seams
to close this century.

In Bosnia. 1993

In Bosnia at 2.30 in the morning
ten women and their girl children
are dragged out of the city.
Other women memorise their names,
the names of the missing.

Me and my Mam stayed inside,
day after night we're together.
She looks like the white meat of pigs
I smell of piss and stale water.

Grandmother says, 'When the sun
goes back to the mountain
the women will start singing.'

How can this be if the tongue
of their joy won't stop bleeding?

The Rescuer

Orpha went into the desert
there she remained.
She required only a little water
and grain that she ate
to stave off her hunger.

She prayed.
Alone in the wind she spoke
first to her spirit then
to the precious eye in the sand.

She wept for her sorrow
which was her frailty
she asked to be strong,
the eye witnessed her pain.

A trickle of water emerged
out of the sand and the sound
was of people moving
and their children

whose tears flowed out
of the eye and their songs
which she could hear
but she couldn't interpret.

The wind said her name
and her sister grew out
of the storm and stayed with her
singing the songs of disquiet
listening to the drone of nations

and she understood
the cry of the homeless
the grief of the bird
whose nest is succunded.

III

Innocence And Regret

Seven times crossed,
once in winter with children,
with my children's children,
with shadows, with the hands
of shadows around me.

In The Beginning There Was Chaos

In the beginning there was chaos –
can you imagine how it was?
I alone was in the sky;
I made much from air,
I felt a huge weight
perhaps tiredness, perhaps despair,

I longed to be apart
from my creation,
to rest as I had before.
I wanted no part of earth
yet part of me was there,
a moiety of self but different

more gentle. Tell me
where you were – from where
did you see my hand
sweep away the storm
and my finger stroke
its warmth inside the air?

When the cooled evening
drew in did you see
how the world cowed utterly,
were you suffering?
You see without me you are sad
and though I love you most

of my creation, you are
elusive and will ever be.
Now, no longer sublime
I search the earth to find
such origins you had in me –
desire of my heart

you still absorb me.
How will you know me then?
As someone distant
walking beneath the sky,
the low sun heavy on me
and snow falling,

my face wiped clean
of all I've cried
and your valediction rising.
We will never be the same
since in watching
love so often
you are indifferent,
shards of winter sun
remain, become coolness
between friends,
roots of a beginning
or an end.

Recollection Of A Dream

I recall the house where we lived;
tall columns, my studio,
a bridge in a well planned garden
and the whale in my belly
cries for me –
what is wrong?
Surely after Burri's sacks
there is nothing left to cry for,
surely my dream for you
includes the sky
or have you pulled a blind
across it to remind me
how deep you are inside
and that to love you
I must find
the cave of your disappointment.

*Alberto Burri was an Italian painter who began his career as an artist while in a prisoner-of-war camp. He was best known for his use of blood stained sacking to convey the suffering and tragedy he witnessed there.

Out Of My Blue Mouth

Out of my blue mouth
the right word comes.

I am the code
of my existence
I speak in tongues.

I have an interpreter,
he is severe

out of my blue mouth
words appear.

Last night I changed
into a chimerical thing

a glitter of faces
a chandelier,

I had a million eyes
he has only one

the severe eye
and his tongue

that curls into me
at the magical hour

when the right word
is born
meaningless . . . dour.

White Bridge

A white bridge shines
its arches curve the sky,

in the shade of it
I swim with beggars,

I embrace them like lovers
I kiss their eyes.

In the deep world
I swim with angels

I see the form of them
I touch the space of them

beautiful as stars.

The Tales Of Innocence And Regret

Fruit

Take the sweetest fruit
you have ever tasted
an apple, it's October,
a Worcester Pearmain perhaps,
some fruit as rare
and sweet as that.
Bite out the bad bits
spit them to the ground,
what's left is perfect.

Then a thought occurs,
an old thought, it hurts.
You feel it first
in your fingers
then in your eyes,
now the apple seems heavy,
already you feel
its flesh perish.

Now you want to carry
the Ice Man down the slope
and give him back
to his village.
Instead, you crush the apple
against a wall.
You have lost
its sweetness, forever.

Wind

Remember a pleasing sight,
it's Christmas
every house has a tree
every shop is alight,
you alone are without a family.

Not that you have none
but that you have forgotten them.

Their names are common as shoppers,
yes, exactly their names.
This is a revelation
because you are so young.

And if you dream
in that miracle night you dream
without them.
Without history or lineage
and all that's in your future
you know now
is determined by the wind.

Stones

In the pockets of workers
are collections of stones
and since these are heavy
and drag them down
they move not as swans
but like old coal trains.

The stokers are aged
beyond years,
all that remains
is for them to say goodbye.
Once in snow I waved
to geese flying north,
to say goodbye to days
even to hours.

Of these there is one
who works without tears.
She will remember you to me,
even to air thinning into fire
even to stones.

Grief

In Fontvielle past Mont de Corde
the man Daudet
is cutting again vines of his gift.
He is in the fields
suffused in southern light.
Already he knows his life is complete.

For him
hours are years he imagines,
now he has nothing left to keep.
Nothing personal,
not even a name.
Still he works
and the day fills with a sound of bells.
Behind him night waits patiently,
it sings to itself
a song of grief.

Expulsion. A Foetal Hymn

How terrible it is to be expelled
out of the womb
I was saddened from then on
like I knew no one
and no one knew me
like I felt desolate
you see in there things
were orchestrated differently.

My mother loved my coming
I'd hear her sing bubble music
beautiful
to be so alone inside her
my head its own shape
question shape
my ears still growing
my mouth never open
my lips like cherry blossoms
and my eyes the eyes of heart
of seeing nothing but stars
no not stars
other biochemical things.

I swam and swam
and my Mam loved me
not because I loved her
how would she know anyway
but 'cause I made her feel fine
like a woman should feel –
curled shape at night
to remind me no mother Mam
no one round to love me.

I terrible fright to be expelled
like being thrown out
nothing special about me
no womb to cover over protect
every creature has her skin
and I had mine – it's gone
you see me I'm naked
a stupid sheep sheared naked
yearning massive creature
cold on the hill
lost in fog
no mother Mam
my skin over her memory.

To be back there sometime
like dying like saying
'Why Mam when I loved you
you threw me out and now
I've spent all time
no time searching.'
To be back like your mouth
birthed me
and I'm crawling in again
dying to love you
and you to love me
and we belong
beloved of each other –
never again mother
Mam gone
and me alone knowing no one
and no one knowing me.

Distance

"Everything near becomes distant." Goethe.

Distance, the space between people,
an area vast maybe as oceans,
a vortex into which we plunge
unknowing.
Like the distance of mind
where silent conversation
is a kind of telepathy,
or the distance of love
where we lose completely.

And distance not spatial
where time is accelerated
and I am less like You,
more like something mortal.
Time to is distance
and time repeated,
different as each year
shows the tree to be
something newly created.

A Limb Discarded

In pools at morning
a sad reflection.
The bird's wing is separate.
A nagging pain,
as of something cut away
a limb discarded, an ankle.

Sometimes I have to fly
in even lines, sometimes
I don't make it.
Always the mirage
of strong shoulders, always
movement that confuses

and the pool's radiance
drawn through,
a moment of clarity
a friendship.

Trust My Fortification Of Stone

Trust my fortification of stone
the hard memory,
survivor of winds
that perforate time.

In one agonising moment
see what is already seen,
the hanged bird
the man skulking away . . .

IV

Gericault

The sky sees all
only it knows the truth
hears you call out
from the mountain
sees your terror
and quietens you.

In The Forest Snow Gathers

In the forest snow gathers . . .
A skein of silk lies on stone.
From such quiet inception
the colour red becomes beautiful,
it tears at sky,
it impels, a torrent of petals.

Absence is a cone of silence . . .
The snowshoe hare has fled
the wood, through the pines
its footprints bleed
marking a clear way through.

Snow Causes Eruptions

Snow causes eruptions.
Sometimes silence causes
the fox to scream.
Perhaps just spite
or the horse bolting.

Remember, don't remember.
Sometimes pain crushes
like a roadroller.
Too much un-named.

Wild horses, a thousand
horse and none to ride.
And in the wood
one who waits
sweet dead grasses.

If you paint without mercy
expect a deluge
expect not to be rescued.
What you retain
is a specific time
and closeness.
Already they have
forgotten your name.

First There Is The Question Of Weight

First there is the question of weight.
How much?
So much that one can carry.

The city has many gates,
canals swell, proliferate with leaves.
Everything we do smells of age.

Through time hands draw on things.
Art is;
coming to a place at least
once unoccupied
and pouring in.

The way you see it matters most.
The way you draw on yourself,
then like this when spring is past
the way it engulfs you.

What Cannot Be Seen

What cannot be seen remains
when the water leaves.
What you recall is almost real,
your hand on her forehead
your hand drawing a brow.

Then in days gradually a depth,
water's dullness and reeds.
Is she the one who came
yesterday who comes again?

Truth is to be immersed.
First in water
then the sorrow field.

Believe Me There Is Only Wind

Believe me there is only wind
and a carcass moon . . .
You have learned so little
even to go back would be difficult.

Look for a place,
find a clearing among trees
where old ones sing.

Believe me there is no one
so homeless
so much without dreams.

If you would show me
a way through
along footpaths lined with trees

I would find a place for us.
See how well I recognise the streets
how fiercely I chew the moon.

I Glimpsed The Moon

(for Maeve)

I glimpsed the moon,
clear bright thing that is part
of you lost among tall pines.

We are far away being so alike.
Barely free but deep green
as the pool that becomes light

in days, days that open out
to fan the world.
See me toward a certain path

strewn with last winter's death.
Life dying cries
from a pool of forgiveness

where breath on breath
layers my sorrow.
Now's the deepest time,

I wander without pain
without even a place
where I can say,

'This is a point wherein
I contain myself'
before and after

like a wind lost
on the same path circling
the world forever.

No rest, no peace
except in that strange light
that opens into days

and blows past
and is the music
and the soul together.

Eyes

(for Richard)

It is never too late to say
before leaving perhaps,
nothing is the same.

The tree transforms.
It could be an angel,
it could be someone
whose name evades you,
it could be the last
of the verticals
in a landscape of burials.

First, let the angel open
as in mornings
when dawn explodes.
This one is a child
in dream, in memory.

It is never too much to say
at evening,
what you did yesterday
you will do again.

Returning,
as when the known voice
is heard in half light
calling you in
and you stumble forward
realising,
a solitary brightness.

It is never too much to say
in the dark night,
our blindness threatened
to kill.

What I lost sight
of will be found again.
The stars that are your eyes
the green brown of autumn.

The singers are silent
spring's growing away from you.
Time to say
this is the hours change
innocent and guilty together
our hands shining clean.

Notes

Homecoming was originally part of *Voices and Light*, a performance by the Fourfront Poets in the Belltable, Limerick, in December 1989.

Waterfall. The Song Of Kunapipi. Kunapipi was the mother goddess of the aboriginal tribes of northern Australia. During the ancestral period she gave birth to men and women as well as creating the natural species. A *rainbow serpent* went before her in order to prepare her way. (A Dictionary of World Mythology.)

Gericault. The first six poems in this section are based on the life of Theoadore Gericault the French 17th century painter. He is perhaps best known for his painting, *The Raft Of The Medusa*. He visited England and later illustrated many of Byron's poems. Lines 10 and 11 of the poem *Snow Causes Eruptions* are taken from the poem *Mazeppa* by Byron. Gericault died aged 34.